Mr McGREEVY'S ABSOLUTE HOWLERS

Mr McGREEVY'S ABSOLUTE HOWLERS

Norman McGreevy

ALLEN&UNWIN

First published in 2006

Allen & Unwin
83 Alexander Street
Crows Nest NSW 2065
Australia

Phone:	(61 2) 8425 0100
Fax:	(61 2) 9906 2218
Email:	info@allenandunwin.com
Web:	www.allenandunwin.com

National Library of Australia
Cataloguing-in-Publication entry:

McGreevy, Norman.
Mr McGreevy's absolute howlers.

ISBN 978 174114 858 9
ISBN 1 74114 858 8.

1. English language - Humor. 2. Children - Language. 3. English language - Errors of usage. I. Title.

428.00207

Illustrations by Zoë Sadokierski
Set in Minion Pro 16pt by Zoë Sadokierski
Printed in Australia by McPherson's Printing Group

10 9 8 7 6 5 4 3 2 1

CONTENTS

I

Dear Reader,

If you have picked up this book then I trust we are kindred spirits, bound together by our collective outrage at the ways in which the youth of today are mangling the English language; chewing up words and spitting them out until, like a cashmere cardigan after it's been through the spin cycle, their beauty and power are diminished.

Be warned, your complicity in reading this book may see you accused of pedantry. Perhaps even cruelty. Old fashioned fuddy-duddiness. Be brave in the face of such taunts. I for one am proud to be a curmudgeon. I never vote for anyone. I vote against. I believe we have to save the earth from evangelical environmentalists and dubious politicians who like bananas start off green, turn yellow and then become rotten.

Nothing on TV, except documentaries about the eating habits of the common earwig, even remotely interests me, health food makes me sick, my favourite animal is bacon and the sight of any actor spouting serious opinions, on any topic, I find so completely laughable I have to go and lie down.

And so it is with curmudgeonly pride that I say we must stand united in our righteous protection of literary correctness. For if we allow this state of affairs to continue we will lose not only our future but our past.

It is outrageous, for example, that little Johnny in 5G should think that 'Germany's William the Second had a chimp on his shoulder and therefore had to ride his horse with one hand' or that Catherine in 6A should truly believe 'Joan of Arc was Noah's sister'. This sort of thing, although inadvertently and deeply humorous, can not go unchecked.

And then there is the smut. When asked what he did in his summer holidays, Jack wrote: 'While rowing up river I slumped over the whores in a state of physical exhaustion.' This boy is not yet even out of long shorts.

I blame the well-known fact that students can't read, write or spell on an education system where sharing feelings is more important than learning to achieve. A fellow curmudgeon I know likes to say that reading most of his students' English essays feels like watching somebody use a Stradivarius to pound nails. I couldn't agree more. In fact I only wish I'd said it myself.

I also blame television, of course. The influence of soap operas and movie gangsters is apparent in students' use of informal language in their essays, referring to Charles V as 'Philip's dad' or reporting that Luther had 'bad-mouthed' the Pope and the Gestapo 'did over' those who 'bad-mouthed' Hitler.

But it doesn't stop there. What about this new fangled business of text messaging. Cul8r. Do these children read anything that isn't on a screen? Is it any wonder Mary thinks 'the appendix is a part of a book for which nobody ever found a use'?

I can offer only one consolation to soothe the blisters of our torment. Humour. The only good that can come of the murder of proper English language usage is laughter. And you will laugh my friends.

This leads me to one of the problems with the collection of Howlers you hold in your hand. The reader may be tempted to read too many of them at one sitting. This is a mistake. It can be done, but it leaves the reader limp with laughter, much like over-exercising, and it's really not worth doing, just for the sake of saying you have done it. Take it easy. Spread it out over the course of a week. Assimilate the benefits little by little. I'd recommend carrying it with you, dipping into it, and turning down the page corners, for a quick pick me up.

While I am sure many of the Howlers in this collection have been cut and polished over the years, and many may doubt the authenticity of some of the more fanciful, there has been no need for invention. Indeed, any attempt at invention soon stands out from their natural and uncontrived feel. There is a great feeling of satisfaction to know that you have produced a book that is guaranteed to bring laughter and amusement, and now even better health, to so many people. This compilation, *Mr McGreevy's Absolute Howlers*, drawn from many thousands of

Howlers in exam papers and student essays, takes the very best to show that this well established tradition is very much alive and well. As for the preservation of the fine traditions of correct punctuation, sentence structure, and factual accuracy, we can only hope and pray for a turnaround in this alarming trend towards casual and sloppy language.

As you start out on your crusade, fear not the cries of the unrighteous—'Why are you always such a terrible curmudgeon? Go out and have some fun, get a life' or more pointedly 'Shut up, and don't ever come to my house again, you miserable old bastard'. Forgive them, for they know not what they do. Ignoramuses.

Norman McGreevy
September 2006

School Days

He closed his eyes in a gesture of despair; he contorted his face, praying for strength, and then lifted his leg, aiming towards the horizon.

He was a man of about 35 years of age, looked twenty and was forty.

Pails and bowels were
flung all over the plaice.

Walking along the country lane,
with my feet in the stirrups.

The dream in every newlywed
couple's head is to marry.

If he is not checked at the right age he will gradually develop into a vandal, and it will not be long before he is a magistrate.

If a tree falls in the dessert, does it make a sound?

All the crew were taken into custardy.

Upstairs, on the front of
the house, is the bathroom.
This comprises of one bath,
sink unit and toilet with enough
room to tuck one's toes in.

People were running all over
the place, the boys in shorts and
the girls in hysterics.

We had a longer holiday than usual this year because the school was closed for altercations.

Girls were typically sent to finishing school where the point was to finish them off.

A hostage is a lady who entertains visitors.

All teachers at our school
are certified.

A polygon is a man
who has many wives.

The headmaster caned me
only on rear occasions.

Writing of the school's old boys
in an essay on the war:
Those that did not go to the war
married, but the stronger ones
started a football team.

Our school is ventilated
by hot currants.

A school teacher leads
a sedimentary life.

Books & Words & Stuff

I c
f J F H
m
o d
A n
e x
k R K B
c
M y Q
g
N E a
w
Z
j
t
i b h
l
q
V

A fairy tale is something that never happened a long time ago.

She worked herself up into an inarticulate comma.

Lady Jane Grey said she was content with her books, so she was beheaded.

The word trousers is an uncommon noun because it is singular at the top and plural at the bottom.

The appendix is a part of a book for which nobody ever found a use.

ink

Ovid wrote a poem called the 'Medea' which was lost fortunately.

Writing at the same time as Shakespeare was Miguel Cervantes. He was Donkey Hote.

Polonius was a mythical sausage.

Shakespeare married Anne Hathaway, but he mostly lived at Windsor with his merry wives. This is quite usual with actors.

Achilles appears in 'The Illiad', by Homer. Homer also wrote the 'Oddity', in which Penelope was the last hardship that Ulysses endured on his journey.

Homer wrote the 'Oddity'. Actually, Homer was not written by Homer but by another man of that name.

Voltaire invented electricity and also wrote a book called 'Candy'.

John Milton wrote 'Paradise Lost'. Then his wife died and he wrote 'Paradise Regained'.

An epitaph is a short sarcastic poem.

Poetry is when every line starts with a capital letter and doesn't reach the right side of the page.

Lord Byron wrote epics and swam the Hellespont. In between he made love drastically.

In Ibsen's 'Ghosts', Oswald dies of congenial syphilis.

The brave knight was swallowed up by the awful abbess that yawned all of a sudden in front of him.

Shakespeare lived in Windsor with his merry wives, writing tragedies, comedies and errors.

A relative pronoun is a family pronoun, such as 'mother', 'brother', 'uncle'.

Letters in sloping type are in hysterics.

Emphasis in reading is putting more distress in one place than another.

An abstract noun is one that cannot be heard, seen, touched, or smelt.

Brutus was a tragic hero in spite of dying in the end.

In conclusion we may say that Shylock was greedy, malicious, and indeed, entirely viscous.

Geography

A consonant is a large piece of land surrounded by water.

A glazier is a man who runs down mountains.

The general direction of the Alps is straight up.

The Wholey Roman Empire amazed many when it was found in Germany.

The population of Sydney is a bit too thick.

Britain has a temporary climate.

In some rocks there are to be found the fossil footprints of fishes.

The Andes are a race of people living in North America.

The principal exports of Sweden are hired girls.

The Dutch people use water power to drive their windmills.

Coal is decayed vegetarians.

The climate of the island
is wet but embracing.

A Native American calls his
wife a squaw and his children
squawkers.

History

King Arthur lived in the Age of Shivery.

My favorite myth was Jason and the Huguenots.

Socrates died from an overdose of wedlock.

In the Olympic games, Greeks ran races, jumped, hurled the biscuits, and threw the java.

The Persians outnumbered the Greeks because they had more men.

The wife of a duke is a dukky.

Helen of Troy launched a thousand ships with her face.

Alexander the Great conquered Persia, Egypt and Japan. Sadly he died with no hairs.

Another Greek myth was Jason and the Golden Fleas.

The Epicureans and the Synthetics believed 'If you can't play with it, why bother?

Joan of Arc was burnt to a steak.

Queen Elizabeth never married, she had a peaceful reign.

Magna Carta provided that no man should be hanged twice for the same offence.

Joan of Arc was Noah's sister.

When Elizabeth exposed herself before her troops, they all shouted, 'hurrah'. Then her navy went out and defeated the Spanish Armadillo.

Medieval people were violent. Murder during this period was nothing. Everybody killed somebody.

During the Middle Ages
the Surfs were dentured
and bonded to the ground.

Two hundred years of rule by
the Tarts explains why Russia
became so backward.

The Turks manicured
the pilgrims.

Victims of the Black Death
grew boobs on their necks.

The King wore a scarlet robe
trimmed with vermin.

K

Ivan the Terrible started life as a child, a fact that troubled his later personality.

Arrested witches were torchured until they told a story. The worst of this could be the rack or burning with hot porkers. Some women were made to endure the ducking stool.

In the middle of the 18th century, all the morons moved to Utah.

The German Emperor's lower passage was blocked by the English.

The War of the Spanish Succession ended in a drawl.

The British used mostly Aztec troops to do their fighting at Gallipoli.

Germany's William the Second had a chimp on his shoulder and therefore had to ride his horse with one hand.

In 1937 Lenin revolted Russia after the Germans sent him home in a soiled train.

Clive committed suicide three times and the third time they sent him to India.

Louis XVI was gelatined to death.

The French Revolution was caused by overcharging taxis.

Henry VIII by his own efforts increased the population of England by 40 000.

Hitler's instrumentality of terror was the Gespacho.

When things didn't go as planned, Stalin used the peasants as escape goats.

Hitler committed suicide in his bunk.

Politics

1

When Caesar was assassinated, he is reported to have said 'Me too, Brutus!'

King John ground the people down under heavy taxis.

Karl Marx's Communist Fiesta was very important.

Machiavelli who was often unemployed, wrote 'The Prince' to get a job with Richard Nixon.

Laissez-faire meant 'let the farmers pay the taxes'.

A caucus is a sort of big parrot that has been taught to swear.

President Carter faced the 'Iran Hostess Crisis'.

The USSR and the USA became global in power, but Europe remained incontinent.

When Gorbachev became top Russian the USSR shifted to a new planet of existance.

Animals

Sharks were infesting the area, and one of them was a non-swimmer.

A Mayor is a he horse.

Benjamin Franklin discovered electricity by rubbing two cats backwards and declared, 'A horse divided against itself cannot stand'.

An armadillo is an
ornamental shrub.

To keep milk from turning sour:
keep it in the cow.

Marsupials are
poached animals.

The home of the swallow
is the stomach.

Anthroapologists have proved
that when animals were not
available the people ate
nuts and barrys.

Herrings go about
the sea in shawls.

A monkey has a reprehensible tail.

Frogs have webbed feet for swimming but, like ducks, these are fine to walk on.

Men are mammals and women are femammals.

The hydra gets its food by descending upon its prey and pushing it into its mouth with its testicles.

The adder is a poisonous snack.

An octogenarian is an animal which has eight young at birth.

One horsepower is the amount of energy it takes to drag a horse 500 feet in one second.

The largest mammals are to be found in the sea because there is nowhere else to put them.

Science & Medicine

Some of the patients were plastered, and some were hanging from the ceiling.

For fractures: to see if the limb is broken, wiggle it gently back and forth.

For snakebites: bleed the wound and rape the victim in a blanket for shock.

If anyone should faint put her head between the knees of the nearest medical man.

Later on the doctor gave him piles to relief him his pain.

Although the patient had never been fatally ill before, he woke up dead.

A circle is a figure with 0 corners and only one side.

A phlegmatic person is one who has chronic bronchitis.

The liver is an infernal organ.

Nuclear activity causes distortions in the jeans of women.

A city purifies its water supply by filtering the water and forcing it through an aviator.

A major discovery was made by Mary Leaky, who found a circle of rocks that broke wind.

Nets are holes surrounded by pieces of string.

Crude oil is a vicious substance.

The Scientific Revolution developed a suppository of knowledge which greatly helped later generations.

If you cross XY and XX chromosones, you get XX (female), YY (male) and XY (undecided).

An advantage of an organism having both sexual and asexual reproduction in its life-cycle: twice as much reproducing.

Al Chemy was a man who discovered chemistry.

If teeth are not cleaned, plague is the result.

Vacuums are nothings. We only mention them to let them know we know they are there.

In biology today,
we digested a frog.

To germinate is to become
a naturalised German.

The earth makes a resolution every 24 hours.

Rainbows are just to look at, not to really understand.

Pine is an example of a carnivorous tree.

Clouds are high flying fogs.

Clouds just keep circling the earth around and around. And around. There is not much else to do.

Methane, a greenhouse gas, comes from the burning of trees and cows.

Parallel lines never meet unless you bend one or both of them.

Music

S.O.S. is a musical term
meaning 'same only softer'.

I know what a sextet is,
but I'd rather not say.

When not working in the
church, Bach composed pieces
on a spinster in his home.

Refrain means don't do it. A refrain in music is the part you better not try to sing.

Stradivarius is an imaginary prehistoric animal.

John Sebastian Bach died from 1750 to the present.

Anyone who can read all the instrument notes at the same time gets to be the conductor.

Handel was half German half Italian and half English. He was very large.

1 2 3

You should always say celli when you mean there are two or more cellos.

When electric currents go through them, guitars start making sounds. So would anybody.

Question: What are kettle drums called? Answer: Kettle drums.

Question: Is the saxophone a brass or a woodwind instrument? Answer: Yes.

One semibreve equals two minions and one crochet four semi-skews.

Religion

The masculine of vixen is vicar.

Peat was made out of moses.

The result of the Reformation was that the people could choose either to be Catholics or pugilists.

The Jews were a proud people, but always had trouble with unsympathetic Genitals.

Zorroastrologism was founded by Zorro. This was a duelist religion.

The seventh commandment is 'Thou shall not admit adultery'.

One of the opossums was
St Mathew he was also a taximan.

One of Jacobs sons, Joseph,
gave refuse to the Israelites.

Solomon was very fond of
animals because he had
300 porcupines.

Solomon had 300 wives and 700 cucumbers.

David was a Hebrew king skilled at playing the liar. He fought with the Philatelists, a race of people who lived in Biblical times.

The Papal Bull was a mad bull kept by the Pope in the Inquisition to trample on Protestants.

Greek religion was polyphonic. Featured were gods such as Herod, Mars, and Juice.

The entire city of Constantinople rose up with a tremendous ejaculation every time the Christan Emperor Constantine came.

The Philistines are islands in the Pacific.

The message came to Abraham that he should bear a son, and Sarah, who was listening behind the door, laughed.

A republican is a sinner mentioned in the bible.

Paraffin is the next order of angels above seraphims.

God's Own Country is Heaven.

Everyone was pleased when Jesus healed the paralytic man, except Simon who had to pay to have the roof mended.

The chief missile of the Church of England is the Prayer Book.

The end of the World will
mark a turning point
in everyone's life.

Moses received the Ten
Commandments on two
stones, and these he impressed
upon the people.

As the creator cools it hardens.

The natives of Macedonia
did not believe in Paul,
so he got stoned.

Pompeii was destroyed by an
overflow of saliva from
the Vatican.

Judyism had one big God
named 'Yahoo'.

An angry Martin Luther nailed
ninety five theocrats to
a church door.

Oliver Cromwell had a large red
nose, but under it were deeply
religious feelings.

Possession by spirits means
feeling like the devil.

R-Rated

As he walked through
his room he heard the sound
of heavy breeding.

When the wedding was over
the bridegroom clasped his
loved one tight in his arms,
while the little organ began
to swell and fill the room.

109

While rowing up river I slumped over the whores in a state of physical exhaustion.

Promiscuous behaviour leaves them with a problem behind.

She took me indoors
and called her husband;
he was very practical
and gave me a nightdress
and some hot soup, and
told me to lie down
in his bed.

III

In the Middle Ages
people lived in mud huts with
rough mating on the floor.

The nineteenth century
was when people stopped
reproducing by hand and
started reproducing
by machine.

Madame Pompadour gained
in power while being
placed under the king.

Merchants appeared and roamed
from town to town exposing
themselves and organizing big
fairies in the countryside.

These peace-loving animals start their life as small, furry balls, and they grow up and with any luck will find a mate, and have small, furry balls themselves.

The Mona Liza was the most beautiful woman ever to be laid on canvas.

115

I secretly entered the boat
with a feeling of suspiciousness.
I hid myself under the bed of a
woman. Doing all this without
the consent of the woman,
I managed to overcome my
nervousness by introducing
myself to her in the dark, and
gained full advantage of it.

A wife should be understanding
and loving and bare
with her husband.

A census taker is a man who
goes from house to house
increasing the population.

Gonads are a tribe of
wandering desert people.

Roman girls who did not marry
could become Vestigal Virgins,
a group of women who were
dedicated to burning
the internal flame.

4/25

She lay there semi-naked,
semi-conscious, and
semi-hopeful.

A gelding is a stallion who has
his tonsils taken out so he would
have more time to himself.

Early Egyptian women often wore a garment called a calasiris. It was a sheer dress which started beneath the breasts which hung to the floor.

Adolescence is the stage between puberty and adultery.